Blythefield-isms

Blythefield-isms

A GUIDE TO UNDERSTANDING BHBC VOCABULARY

Edited by Pete Ford

Blythefield-isms :: A Guide to Understanding BHBC Vocabulary

Cover designer :: Sarah Molegraaf

Interior designer :: Pete Ford

General editor :: Pete Ford

Second Printing, 2018

ISBN-13: 978-0-9863012-2-3

Some concepts are adapted from *True North* by Gary and Lisa Heim

Some concepts are adapted from *The Marriage Builder* by Dr. Larry Crabb

TABLE OF CONTENTS

EDITOR'S NOTE

My family started attending Blythefield Hills Baptist Church the week before I turned one, so I have grown up learning the Sunday School answers, then anticipating the next youth trip. I remember Awana games and Virtual City's Streets and Sewers. I've studied the carpet patterns in each hallway and have vacuumed most of them.

Blythefield is what I know. Growing up, my parents told me there is something unique about the culture of Blythefield. One of the best things about Blythefield is that we have a vocabulary. These terms and phrases allow us to start each conversation a half-step ahead, already with some common ground. While we do not hold our particular phrases as ultimate, they provide a starting point for conversations.

Whether you are brand-new or a veteran of Blythefield, I hope this book will help you understand the language more clearly. I pray this will build our unity within the Body of Christ.

While I know Blythefield is far from perfect, God is doing a work here. Despite the brokenness of people, Christ's Bride, the Church, has stood for two thousand years. God has a mission so much greater than our weakness or strength. May the people of Blythefield be characterized by our love for God and others; may we be led by God's Word, filled with His Spirit, surrounded by His people, on His mission.

– Pete Ford, summer 2017

CORE TERMINOLOGY

Mission :: Always Making Disciples

Based on The Great Commission in Matthew 28:19-20a:

"Go therefore and make disciples of all nations, baptizing them in the name of the Father and of the Son and of the Holy Spirit, teaching them to observe all that I have commanded you."

Disciple :: A wholehearted follower of Jesus.

Our job is to allow the Gospel to go forth with clarity and be lived out with sincerity. *Redemptive relationships* are essential for this.

Edification and Evangelism

Another way we say this is that our job is to assist in getting as many people as He desires to Heaven in the best shape possible.

Edification and Evangelism (E and E) :: It is important to both bring new people into the *Church* and also continue to seek growth and spiritual depth. *Always Making Disciples* means bringing new disciples in and continuing to disciple them for the rest of their lives. You know you "get it" when you give it away.

Vision :: Double Love Command

Double Love Command :: Love God. Love Others.

Adapted from Matthew 22. Jesus summarized the whole Old Testament in this double commandment:

> *"'Love the Lord your God with all your heart and with all your soul and with all your mind.' This is the first and greatest commandment. And the second is like it: 'Love your neighbor as yourself.' All the Law and the Prophets hang on these two commandments." (Matthew 22:37-40 NIV)*

Just like a door needs at least two hinges to hang correctly, the Old Testament hangs on these two commands. The first love depends on the second, and the second love on the first (1 John 2:9-10; 3:14-17; 4:19-21).

Vertical and Horizontal

Vertical Relationship :: Our relationship with God.

Horizontal Relationship :: Our relationships with others.

Life is defined *vertically* before *horizontally*. Without loving the Lord with all our heart, soul, mind and strength, we cannot truly love our neighbor as ourselves.

If we are not living our horizontal relationships of loving our neighbor as ourselves, we are missing something key in our vertical relationship with God. If we deny this, we are deceiving ourselves (1 John 2:9).

Values :: Worship, Learn, Connect, Serve, Give and Reach

Taken from a study of the early Church in the book of Acts, these six values shape how we operate as a church to live out our mission and vision. First, we worship God and connect with other believers to continue learning. As we are poured into we pour out through serving, giving and reaching others with the Gospel.

Worship

While we owe everything to God, we do not worship Him to earn anything. We worship Him out of gratitude for who He is and what He has done. More than just singing, worship is an attitude of response to seeing God and His grace. We gather together weekly to be recharged by the *Word, Spirit and people of God*, then live this lifestyle of worship throughout the whole week.

Learn

God does not allow us to coast but uses His *Word, Spirit and people* to continue growth in us. Learning and growing is a lifelong journey, which grows gratitude for what God has done for us. As we learn, we begin to live it out by *serving* others.

Connect

God created humans to be in relationship with Him, others and ourselves, but the *Fall* corrupted relationships. Because we are hurt most in relationships, God intends that we heal the most within community. We value *transparency* and being known by other believers as we cultivate a place where Truth can be spoken in Love. We offer small groups for all ages to make a large church small.

Serve

Because we have been given so much, we give to others. As we grow in a posture of humility, we live more and more to put others first. Although He does not need us, God has graciously chosen to allow us to play a part in His plan, the *Church*. His Spirit has given each of us unique gifts to discover and share in unique ways.

Give

Because all we have is God's, we can hold our *Time, Talents and Treasure* loosely. He calls us to be stewards of His resources and use them to serve others generously, beginning in our local *Church* then moving out globally (Acts 1:8).

Reach

Also known as Evangelize, *Reach* is spreading the Gospel to the world around us. Because we have been given the truth of salvation through Jesus alone, we have a responsibility to share that with those around us. We begin in our local community then extend out globally. *Reaching* involves three steps:

Pray :: First, we pray for people in our lives who need Jesus.

Act :: We let our loving actions speak as witness of Christ.

Speak :: As we build *redemptive relationships*, we earn the right to speak the Truth in Love, enticing others to enter into God's story by communicating graciously and gently.

131 :: 1 person praying daily for 3 people to come to know the 1 true God.

Word, Spirit and People of God

God reveals Himself to us through General Revelation in creation, but especially in Special Revelation through *His Word*, *His Spirit* and *His people*, to prepare us for His mission. This is the three-legged stool of God's revelation.

The Word of God

The most specific way God has revealed Himself to us is through His Word, the Bible. We value Scripture highly as the very Word of God, our final authority on all things. Because of this, being daily in the Word is important, as is taking time weekly to receive solid Bible-based teaching.

The Spirit of God

As Trinity, God works through His Spirit in the Church, working out the interpretation of His Word in our lives through the Spirit's promptings. Primarily in prayer, we are able to spend time building a relationship with the Creator of the universe.

The People of God

Community is important because God speaks to us through His people. Not only did God create us to *relate*, but His plan for restoration also runs through people. We must be "not neglecting to meet together, as is the habit of some, but encouraging one another, and all the more as you see the Day drawing near" (Hebrews 10:25).

Preferences, Convictions, Absolutes

Personal Preference :: An opinion that is valid but not based on Scripture. Examples include music styles in worship and appropriate clothing for church.

Biblical Conviction :: A doctrinal belief that has Scriptural reasons to back it up, but which is not essential to the faith. Good godly scholars may even debate the meaning of the same Scripture and come to different convictions. Examples include alcohol use and views of the end-times.

Non-Negotiable (Absolute) :: An absolutely clear statement of biblical teaching that all true believers affirm. Examples include the deity of Christ and the infallibility of the Scriptures.

Priorities

If we fill a jar with sand, it's hard to fit the bigger rocks in it. However, if we start with the bigger rocks, and then the smaller pebbles, the sand easily fills in the cracks.

This applies to time-management, as well as doctrine and beliefs. It is often not worth fighting battles over doctrinal minutiae when there are more important discussions to be had. This is why we major on the *Majors*, and minor on the *Minors*.

Minors :: Beliefs that are valid and important but not as vital and core to the faith as the *Majors* are. Examples include music styles, views on alcohol and opinions about the end-times. Anytime we major on a *Minor* by making a small issue big, we distort the Gospel. See also *Majors* :: 13.

	Scripture	Personal Freedom	Tolerance	Dangers
Personal Preference	Silent	Complete	Complete	Offend weaker brother Unnecessary control of others
Biblical Conviction	Debatable	Free to study and to hold one's own interpretation	Pragmatic	Divisiveness within the body of Christ Unfounded dogmatism
Non-Negotiable (Absolute)	Absolutely clear	None on major tenets	None on major tenets	Unwarranted attempts to expand or to shrink this category

The Five Majors

Story

Scripture is full of narrative because story captures our imagination. For example, Jesus often taught through stories and parables.

We must interpret our story within God's story if we are to walk faithfully with Him. See also *Moral Imagination* :: 19.

A compelling and coherent worldview must answer five questions: How did it all begin? What went wrong? Is there a solution? What's our role? How will it all end?

Majors :: The grand narrative of God's story through history reads as the prototype of all storylines, including five major acts. We call these the *Five Majors*. See also *Minors* :: 11.

Creation

"In the beginning, God created the heavens and the earth" (Genesis 1:1). Exactly how God created leaves room for discussion, but the important part is that God called His creation "very good" (Genesis 1:31). In this *Shalom*, God placed people. "So God created man in His own image, in the image of God He created him; male and female He created them" (Genesis 1:27). God created humans in His image, which gives us the responsibility to steward His creation.

Fall

However, Adam and Eve chose to disobey God's command, which brought death into His good creation. Not only does everyone commit sinful acts, but all people have a tendency toward sin through *birth, choice, practice and generational influence*. We can do nothing to save ourselves or earn salvation on our own.

Redemption

But God, in His grace, pursues sinners. Christ achieved salvation for us by living a perfect life in a human body, dying an undeserved death on the cross in our place and resurrecting back to life again. We are called to respond in faith to receive His gift of salvation.

Church

Believers become part of the universal body of Christ as our stories enter God's story. God has graciously called the redeemed to play a role in His redemptive plan. The *Church* is responsible to stand as witness of the Gospel and build each other up, anticipating Christ's return.

New Heaven and Earth

Christ's bride, the *Church*, eagerly anticipates His second coming. God's plan will be completed, and He will separate the sheep from the goats (Matthew 25:31-46). He will make a *New Heaven and Earth*, wiping away all the effects of sin and completely restoring *Shalom* (Isaiah 65:17; 2 Peter 3:13).

Biblical Self-Image

Everything we do, we do according to our self-image. What defines us? We act based on the answer we believe. However, Satan attacks our view of who God is and who we are. The truth of our identity in Christ combats these attacks.

The model of *Son, Servant and Soldier* is not the only correct model. For example, in his book *Sit, Walk, Stand* Watchman Nee uses those three terms to describe this same framework in Ephesians. However, it is important that we have a model to understand our identity in Christ.

We must hold these three identities in the correct order, with balance. Unless we are first secure as children of God, we cannot serve others; we must understand our identity as sons and daughters before we can be freed to serve. Unless we learn a posture of serving, we would hurt others by fighting; we must first learn to serve so we can stand our ground humbly.

Son

First, we must rest in the love of the Father as a *son or daughter*. As Ephesians 1:5 says, "He predestined us for adoption to Himself as sons through Jesus Christ." As a child of God, we learn gratitude for all He has done for us. Jude reminds us to keep ourselves in the love of God (Jude 21). How deeply we understand our sonship will be seen in the quality of our worship, both personally and corporately.

Servant

In Ephesians 4:1, Paul urges us "to walk in a manner worthy of the calling to which you have been called." We can't serve until we have been served. Thankfully, Christ set us an example of the ultimate *servant*. Paul explains, "And walk in love, as Christ loved us and gave Himself up for us, a fragrant offering and sacrifice to God" (Ephesians 5:2). Walking in love looks like serving each other as Christ served us. How deeply we understand our servanthood will be seen in the way we access the power of God.

Soldier

Having rested in the love of the Father and learned to serve others, now we can fight the good fight as a *soldier*. Paul charges us, "Finally, be strong in the Lord and in the strength of His might" (Ephesians 6:10), then lists the full armor of God in the following verses. How deeply we understand our soldiering will be seen in how we understand the purpose of pain and faithfully enter into suffering for the redemption of others.

4 Ps

Our four roles in order, with balance, are:

Person | Partner | Parent | Professional

For students:

Person | Phamily member | Peer | Pupil

SIN

Birth | Choice | Practice | Generational Influence :: We, in our representative Adam, are all sinners. We are sinners by *birth, choice, practice* and *generational influence*. However, God restores us through the new birth, new choices, new practices and new generational influences.

AGENTvictimAGENT :: Although we are victims of sin, we must understand that we are also agents who have sinned against God and others. This is the primary issue: we are agents first and last.

Sex | Power | Money :: The world's big three temptations. All are attempts to grasp for control. Every sin results from a failure to love; at its core, sin is selfish.

Coexistence of Good and Evil :: The great mystery of why God allows evil to exist alongside good (Matthew 13:30) and how He uses evil to bring about good (Romans 8:28).

Passivity

Passivity is the worst of sins because it is unbelief which leads to inaction. Inaction leads to final condemnation for the finally unbelieving (Revelation 21:8) and loss of impact and reward for those who may believe at one level yet live in unbelieving passivity at the level of opportunities to love and serve.

Perfectionism

Perfectionism and its teaching is sin. It's a terrible thing to be right – only. We are not after perfection, but quicker detection and faster resolution. The process is the product we hope for.

51% :: While we will never have 100% pure motives this side of the *New Heaven and Earth*, we aim for 51% or better as we see Christ working in our hearts.

Motives :: Motives are important. Sin is not merely bad actions, but a heart that is bent on rebelling against God. The Spirit in us realigns our loves, as Augustine put it, reordering our heart's desires to place God above all idols. Grace empowers us to not only avoid a list of taboo actions but grows in us a desire to live within God's story. The same action can be sin for one person and not sin for another, because of the state of our hearts.

GRACE

Double Transfer :: In the process of Justification, all our sin is placed upon Christ; all His righteousness is given to us. In 2 Corinthians 5:21, Paul explains, "For our sake He made Him to be sin who knew no sin, so that in Him we might become the righteousness of God."

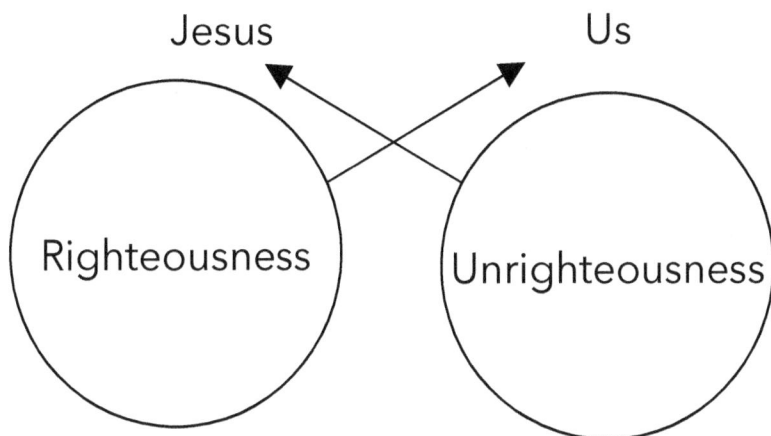

Shalom :: Although often translated as "peace," *Shalom* is much more than the absence of war. *Shalom* is how God created the world to work. Although sin corrupts *Shalom*, God is restoring everything to *Shalom*.

Moral Imagination :: The ability to envision God's story in the midst of circumstances that threaten to take our thinking captive. In the middle of frustration, *Moral Imagination* allows us to move north and see that God has a bigger plan than our immediate circumstances. See also *North and South* :: 23.

Repentance and Faith

Only a crisis (real or perceived) can bring about real change because it forces us to rely on God.

Repentance is turning away from sin. *Faith* is turning toward God. Neither is a one-time decision; both are a continual mindset and a lifestyle. Every day we have to say "no" to some things and "yes" to other things.

The first step toward change is humility. The first beatitude is to be poor in spirit (Matthew 5:3). Under the umbrella of humility, we take the next steps of awareness, ownership, brokenness, surrender and movement.

Repentance is not only feeling bad about sin but taking ownership of it and turning away from it.

Faith is not merely theological assent to doctrines but a daily lived-out pursuit of Christlikeness.

Greatest Day

While we would arrogantly love for everyone to see the five best moments of our lives, how would we feel if the five worst moments were put up on a big screen for all to see?

Greatest Day :: The *greatest day* of your life is the day you face yourself for who you truly are. When we see our own brokenness, we truly see our need for Christ and act more graciously toward other sinful people.

There is nothing automatic in the Christian life. The three stages of the Christian life are easy, hard and impossible. As we grow in Christ, we learn to rely more and more on His strength.

Jesus had no more power to live the Christian life than we do. He gives us the Holy Spirit to empower us to live for Him. (John 14:16-17). And God gives us all we need to be faithful (2 Peter 1:3). There's always enough grace to be faithful.

Tap on the Shoulder :: Every day sin taps us on the shoulder. Opportunity may only knock once, but temptation leans on the doorbell. But thankfully, grace is double-tapping us on the other shoulder – even harder. In Romans 5:20 Paul said, "[B]ut where sin increased, grace abounded all the more."

Theology of Suffering

We don't get to choose what happens to us, but we are responsible for our response. God wants to use pain to grow us in Him (James 1:2-4).

When we live in reality, even bad news can be good news as we allow God to work in us. In the midst of groaning, we can either "go south" by grumbling and grasping or "go north" through gratitude and giving. See also *North and South* :: 23.

Decades of Ds

In our lives, we will hit many walls. God wants us to respond by growing closer to Him instead of more distant. See also *Theology of Suffering* :: 22. This is a general outline of a life through the decades:

20s/Dreams :: "I can change the world."

30s/Disillusionment :: "I can hardly change myself."

Fork in the road :: "At this point, I can either respond to the disillusionment by becoming distant, disengaged and disgruntled, or by cultivating a deep love for Christ."

40s/Depth :: "I need God's help."

50s/Devotion :: "I think I am beginning to understand what Jesus meant when He said without me you can do nothing."

60s+/Delight :: "I know it's not about me but about Him. He is my joy!"

North and South

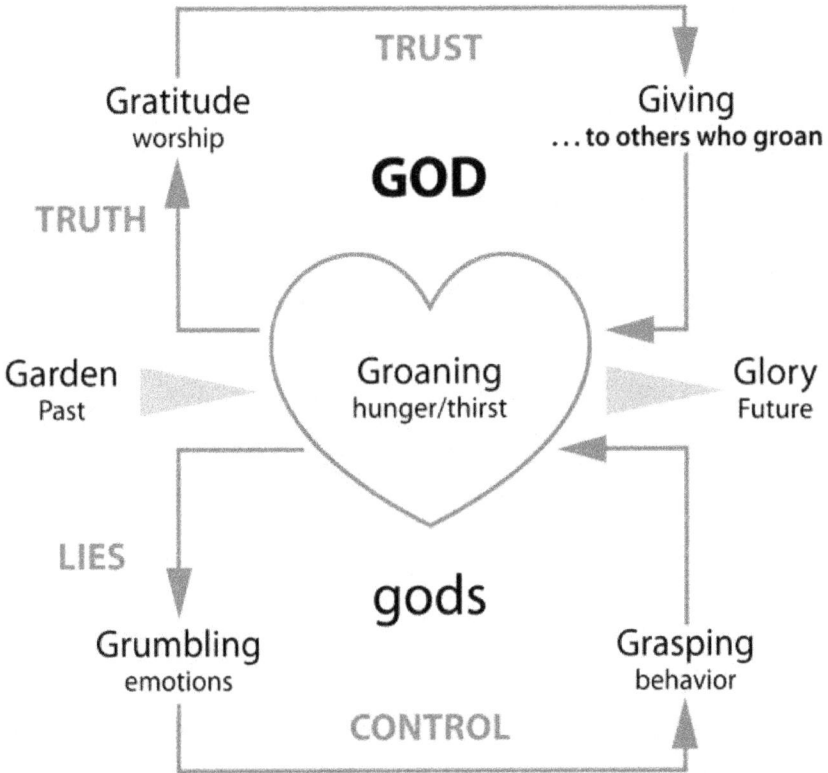

All creation is in the midst of groaning (Romans 8:22-23). While we do not have control over the circumstances that happen to us, we have many choices each day whether to respond by going *north*, toward God, or moving *south*, away from God and toward idols. We go *north* in gratitude for God and respond by serving others. If we grumble and grasp for control, we move *south* and turn our desires into demands.

Tension Theology

Good theology requires tension.

We often look for easy answers to eliminate mystery, confusion and apparent contradiction. When we do this, we water down God's character and Word. Like a guitar string that is best tuned with tension on both ends, God wants us to trust Him as we walk through the middle of tension.

Some examples of these tensions are three-in-one Trinity, Christ as human and divine, Truth and Love, human free will and God's sovereignty and the *Coexistence of Good and Evil*.

We never have the luxury of fighting only one battle at a time. There are always at least two opposing fronts we must battle to live with balance in the tensions of life.

Railroad tracks :: While railroad ties seem like two separate pieces, the farther out we look the two become one. In a similar way, two sides of a tension look separate to us, such as mercy and justice; however, when we look far out they seem to merge together.

Theology of Work

Work is part of God's original *Creation*, before the *Fall*. God created a rhythm of work and rest: work six days and rest one day, a Sabbath. Work connects us with ourselves, God, each other and creation. Through our work, we bring life to the world.

Life-giver | *Power-taker* :: We seek to be life-givers instead of power-takers. We have the power to use words and actions to build others up or tear them down (Ephesians 4:29), so we seek to wield this power responsibly.

Money :: Money is the energy of life, compressed. Money is stored work. The currency we use represents the work we have done, which is easier to barter with than farm animals.

Giving is a response of gratitude. We gratefully tithe at our place of worship because it would be silly to eat at Burger King then drive down the street and pay at McDonald's.

Time | *Talents* | *Treasures* :: God has entrusted each of us to steward these three resources well. He gives us each unique opportunities, gifts and financial resources.

CHURCH

The Church is the greatest idea God ever had. The Church is always underestimated; it is not a sideshow, but a main attraction to the world.

Life would be easy, if it wasn't for other people. The Church is filled with imperfect people. Be a caretaker, not a critic. Paul says to "bear with one another," instead of being a bear to one another (Ephesians 4:2; Colossians 3:13).

The Church is not a country club but a hospital; as the patients are healed, they serve one another. The Church is a lay ministry.

Many seek the kingdom of God, few seek it first (Matthew 6:33).

Judgment starts in the Church; instead of pointing a finger at "those people," we ought to solemnly consider our own sin first (Matthew 7:5).

525 :: A *525* is a highly focused, Christ-centered retreat lasting 24 hours, usually from 5p Friday until 5p Saturday. It is an intentional getaway where we can talk honestly about faith, wounds and identity.

TGPCIAOC :: This is the vision that our emeritus pastor cast for us as he stepped down as senior pastor. He longs to see us be "The greatest praying Church in all of Christendom."

RELATIONSHIPS

We have been hurt most within relationships; God intends that we heal the most within relationships. Since our mission is to be *Always Making Disciples*, every relationship should be a *Redemptive relationship*.

Redemptive relationship :: A relationship that seeks to lead both persons closer to Christ.

A Culture of Transparency

We can only be loved to the degree we are known. We experience Christ when we are fully known at our worst and are still loved. We seek to build a culture where authenticity is rewarded.

We do not lead from our maturity, but from our authenticity. God doesn't use us because we have all the answers, but when we admit that we don't He can use us. By taking off our masks, we build trust with others and encourage them to be known as well.

Life Stages of Relationships

Enchantment :: "I can only see what's good in you."

Pain :: "I can only see what's wrong with you."

Growth :: "I am starting to see what's wrong in me."

Joy :: "I am learning to love others who disappoint me."

Security and Significance

Security :: This refers to our search for value, our thirst for others to love us. However, we find our only true *security* in being in Christ.

Significance :: This refers to our quest to find true purpose in our lives. However, we find our only real *significance* in being in Christ.

We come into relationships with a built-in desire for *Security and Significance*. However, we are often disappointed by the responses we receive. We have four options for responding to that disappointment:

Ignore :: We can act tough to avoid disappointment. However, it is not healthy for us to ignore our emotions.

Achieve :: Another option is to try to find satisfaction in achievement. Ultimately, no matter how much we achieve, we will never be fulfilled.

People :: We will also attempt to meet our needs in relationships with others. However, people will also let us down.

God :: We depend on God to meet our needs. Only in Christ are we truly *Secure and Significant* so we can live responsibly before God and others no matter what. See also *Biblical Self-Image* :: 15.

Platform of Truth

Honoring God in relationships is like a balance beam with an error on either side. We can fall off the *Platform of Truth* in either direction. Both are driven by pride that says we know better than God.

Error 1 :: Rejection or failure tells us we are not valuable.

Error 2 :: We use Christ to ignore pain in relationships.

Stuffing and Dumping

Stuffing :: Often, we *stuff* our wounds and try to ignore them. We hide behind a mask, not allowing others to see what we really feel or who we really are because we live in fear of exposure. This is dangerous because it does not allow us to fully face our wounds.

Dumping :: Other times we take the opposite extreme to legitimize our feelings, *dumping* our feelings on others. Our emotions ought to point us to what is going on under the surface so we can seek God's help, but too often we hurt others by spewing them.

The right way :: We seek to face it and feel it rather than minimize it. When wronged, we allow ourselves to feel the pain, but then move into the situation redemptively instead of letting it fester (Ephesians 4:26). See also *Immediate | Direct | Redemptive* :: 35.

Core Lie and Core Truth

Core Lie

Core Lie :: A deeply held belief that personally attacks our identity and our trust in God. It may take deep reflection on our story to discover it; reflecting on our story in community can help us discover this *Core Lie*.

Growing up in a sinful world, we begin to believe lies about who we are and how God views us. Each of us buys into a unique lie, each stemming from feelings of inadequacy and fear.

Often, these lies are perpetuated by wounds in close relationships, especially within our families. Sinful parents and mentors can wound us either by saying things to us or withholding things from us.

We begin to believe that God is disappointed in us, and consequently, we create coping mechanisms because of our *Core Lies*. It is often helpful to start by identifying and naming the lies we each believe.

For example, we may feel worthless, unwanted or like a loser. Taking it a step further, we begin to label the coping mechanisms we use in response to our lies.

The lie tells me I must always _____ in order to gain acceptance.

The lie tells me I must never _____ in order to avoid rejection.

Core Truth

Core Truth :: The true response in *God's Word* to our unique *Core Lies*.

We must learn how to bury our *Core Lie* with our *Core Truth*. Our pain is real and we must face how others have wounded us, yet we are to remember that we are not *victims*, but *agents* first and last. See also *AGENTvictimAGENT* :: 17.

To replace the lies about who we are and how God sees us, we surround ourselves with the truths God has told us through *His Word, His Spirit* and *His people*. Through this process of replacing the lies with truth, we find our *Security and Significance* in Christ and become free to care more about loving and serving others than protecting ourselves.

Conflict

Conflict is the will of God for relationships. The quality of any relationship depends on how it handles conflict. Marriage and other relationships are not intended to make us happy but holy.

The issue is never the issue :: There is much more going on under the surface, like an iceberg. What is the question behind the question? When we see the red flags of emotions such as anger, we pause and ask ourselves what insecurities sit beneath the symptoms on the surface-level.

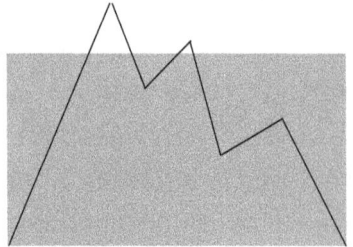

Balance of Truth and Love

We are called to speak the Truth in Love (Ephesians 4:15). We can love others on our own, and we can speak truth on our own. But the balance of speaking Truth in Love can only be achieved through the Spirit's help.

We cannot grow beyond Love, we must grow in it. Truth is the platform to get there.

Forgiveness :: "Fairness" does not bring true forgiveness. Responding out of gratitude for God's forgiveness frees us to truly forgive wrongs committed against us.

IDR

Immediate | Direct | Redemptive (IDR) :: In our sin, we often let wounds fester and gossip. Instead, we seek to directly approach the person who hurt us as soon as we can (Ephesians 4:26-27), humbly seeking the restoration of the relationship.

If your brother sins against you, go and tell him his fault, between you and him alone. If he listens to you, you have gained your brother. But if he does not listen, take one or two others along with you, that every charge may be established by the evidence of two or three witnesses. If he refuses to listen to them, tell it to the church. (Matthew 18:15-17a)

OIC

Observation | Interpretation | Clarification (OIC) :: When we see an issue in another believer, we humbly come, seeking to listen rather than be heard. *OIC* can offer a framework to phrase our concern. "Lately I have seen you X. It seems to me that might be Y. Can you help me understand what's going on in your mind?"

Appropriate Boundaries

Circles of Influence and Concern

Our *Circle of Influence* includes the area in life we have control over. Our *Circle of Concern* includes things that affect us, but which we don't have direct control over.

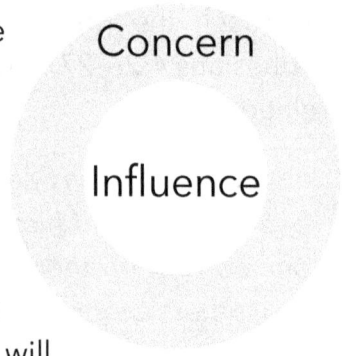

Concern

Influence

If we mistakenly focus on our *Circle of Concern* that we can't change, our *Circle of Concern* will begin to crowd out our *Circle of Influence*, shrinking the spheres where we actually have influence.

Desire | Goal

Desire :: A thing we want but can't achieve on our own. Our response is to surrender desires to God through prayer.

Goal :: An objective under our control. Our response is to determine the steps needed to achieve this goal and begin moving forward.

Instant Gratification | Delayed Gratification

Instant Gratification :: Demanding that we get what we want immediately.

Delayed Gratification :: The ability to patiently wait for what we desire because we know it will be better.

Main Sinful Patterns

Men

The main sinful pattern of men is the avoidance of leadership through blame-shifting. We can see this in the story of Adam in the Garden of Eden. Genesis 3:6 says he was standing right there and did not speak up to remind his wife of God's command not to eat the fruit. A few verses later, he hid out of fear then shifted the blame to his wife (Genesis 3:12).

Two main strategies are to hide in fear or explode in anger. We find ourselves somewhere on this continuum:

Little Boy | Nice Guy | Driven Guy | Macho Jerk

Redeemed masculinity is a balance between strength and involvement.

Women

The main sinful pattern of women is the manipulation of relationships through pressure. We can see this in the story of Eve in the Garden of Eden. She desired to control her husband, according to Genesis 3:16.

Two main strategies are to use service to manipulate or to distance ourselves from relationships. We find ourselves somewhere on this continuum:

Little Girl | Busy Bee | Party Girl | Tough Girl

Redeemed femininity is a balance between softness and competence.

GLOSSARY/INDEX

Conflict :: The will of God for relationships :: 34

Connect :: Because we were created to live in relationships, we value fellowship within community; one of the six Values, *which see* :: 8

Conviction; *also called* Biblical Conviction :: A doctrinal belief with Scriptural reasons backing it up, but not essential to the faith :: 11

Core Lie :: A belief that personally attacks our identity and trust in God; *see also* Core Truth :: 32

Core Truth :: The response in *God's Word* to our unique Core Lies; *see also* Core Lie :: 33

Creation :: God created everything; one of the Five Majors, *which see* :: 13

Decades of Ds :: As we hit walls in our lives, God wants us to grow closer to Him instead of rejecting Him :: 22

Desire :: A thing we want but can't achieve on our own. Our response: pray about desires and surrender them to God; *see also* Goal :: 36

Delayed Gratification :: The ability to patiently wait for what we desire because we know it will be better; *see also* Instant Gratification :: 36

Disciple :: A wholehearted follower of Jesus :: 5

Double Love Command :: Our vision to love God and love others :: 6

Double Transfer :: All our sin is placed upon Christ; all His righteousness is given to us :: 19

Dumping :: An unhealthy pattern of relating that includes oversharing emotions; *see also* Stuffing :: 31

Edification and Evangelism; *also called* E and E :: Our dual focus on discipling brand-new believers as well as continuing to disciple believers more deeply :: 5

Evangelize; *see* Reach; one of the six Values, *which see* :: 9

Faith :: Turning toward God; both a Mindset and a Lifestyle; *see also* Repentance :: 20

Fall :: The tragic event that invited sin into the world, causing the downfall of humanity; one of the Five Majors, *which see* :: 14

Five Majors; *see* Majors :: 13

Forgiveness :: "Fairness" does not bring true forgiveness :: 34

Give :: We worship God by being generous stewards of what He has given us; one of the six Values, *which see* :: 8

Goal :: An objective under our control we can achieve by responsible actions; *see* also Desire :: 36

Greatest day :: The greatest day of your life is the day you face yourself for who you truly are :: 21

Horizontal Relationship :: Our relationship with others; *see also* Vertical :: 6

Iceberg :: The issue is never the issue; there is much more going on under the surface :: 34

IDR :: A framework for how to respond when we have been wounded; Immediate | Direct | Redemptive :: 35

Instant Gratification :: Demanding that we get what we want immediately; *see also* Delayed Gratification :: 36

Issue is never the issue :: There is much more going on under the surface, like an iceberg :: 34

Learn :: Our life-long pursuit of growth in Christ; one of the six Values, *which see* :: 7

Life-giver :: We have the power to use our words and actions to build each other up; *see also* Power-taker :: 25

Life Stages of Relationships :: Enchantment | Pain | Growth | Joy :: 29

Main Sinful Patterns :: The primary sinful habits of men and women :: 37

Main Sinful Pattern: Men :: Avoidance of leadership through blame shifting :: 37

Main Sinful Pattern: Women :: Manipulation of relationships through pressure :: 37

Majors; *also called* Five Majors :: The five acts in God's story of history: Creation | Fall | Redemption | Church | New Heaven and Earth, *which see* :: 13

Minors :: Beliefs that are not as vital and core as the Majors, *which see* :: 11

Mission :: Always Making Disciples, *which see* :: 5

Money :: Stored work; the energy of life compressed; *see also* Theology of Work :: 25

Moral Imagination :: The ability to envision God's story in the midst of circumstances that threaten to take our thinking captive :: 19

Motives :: Motives are everything; the state of our hearts matters more than just actions; *see also* 51% :: 18

New Heaven and Earth :: The consummation of God's plan of redemption and restoration; the end-point of history; one of the Five Majors, *which see* :: 14

Non-Negotiable; *also called* Absolute :: A doctrine that is essential to the historic Christian faith :: 11

North :: Turning toward God in difficult circumstances; *see also* South :: 23

OIC :: A framework to approach a believer who we see living in sin; Observation | Interpretation | Clarification :: 35

Passivity :: The terrible sin of unbelief, leading to loss of opportunities :: 19

Perfectionism :: It's a terrible thing to be right – only; we're not after perfection, but quicker detection and faster resolution :: 18

Personal Preference; *see* Preference :: 11

People of God :: God speaks to us through other believers, members of His Church; *see also* Word of God *and* Spirit of God :: 10

Platform of Truth :: Honoring God in relationships is like a balance beam with an error on either side; *see also* Stuffing and Dumping :: 31

Power-taker :: We have the power to use our words and actions to tear each other down; *see also* Life-giver :: 25

Pray | Act | Speak; *see* Reach :: 9

Preference; *also called* Personal Preference :: A valid but not Scripturally-based opinion, such as worship styles :: 11

Priorities :: When the most important things are treated as important, less important things will find their place :: 11

Railroad tracks :: The farther out we look, two sides of a tension merge into one :: 24

Reach; *also called* Evangelize :: Sharing the Gospel with others within the context of redemptive relationships, *which see*; *see also* Pray | Act | Speak :: 9

Redemption :: God's plan to rescue the world from sin and restore Shalom, *which see*; one of the Five Majors, *which see* :: 14

Redemptive relationships :: Relationships that seek to lead us both closer to Christ :: 29

Repentance :: Turning away from sin; both a Mindset and a Lifestyle; *see also* Faith :: 20

Security and Significance :: Our longing for Security and Significance is dissatisfied until we find true rest in God alone :: 30

Servant; *see* Son | Servant | Soldier :: 16

Serve :: One way we worship God is by serving Him through serving others; one of the six Values, *which see* :: 8

Sex | Power | Money :: The world's big three temptations, each is an attempt to grasp for control :: <u>17</u>

Shalom :: More than the absence of war, Shalom is a picture of the world entirely whole, how God intended it to be :: <u>19</u>

Significance; *see* Security and Significance :: <u>30</u>

Six Values; *see* Values :: <u>7</u>

Soldier; *see* Son | Servant | Soldier :: <u>16</u>

Son | Servant | Soldier :: A biblical self-image model :: <u>15</u>

South :: Turning away from God in difficult circumstances; *see also* North :: <u>23</u>

Spirit of God :: Jesus sent us the Holy Spirit as a counselor and guide we communicate with primarily through prayer; *see also* Word of God *and* People of God :: <u>10</u>

Story :: Scripture is full of narrative because story captures our imagination :: <u>13</u>

Stuffing :: An unhealthy pattern of relating that involves hiding our emotions from others; *see also* Dumping :: <u>31</u>

Tap on the Shoulder :: Every day sin taps us on the shoulder, but Grace also does :: <u>21</u>

Tension Theology :: Good theology requires tension; God wants us to trust Him as we walk through the middle of tension :: <u>24</u>

TGPCIAOC :: Our emeritus pastor's vision for us to be "The greatest praying Church in all of Christendom" :: <u>27</u>

Theology of Suffering :: When we trust God, we can rely on Him in the midst of pain :: <u>22</u>

Theology of Work :: Work is part of God's original creation, before the Fall ::

Time | Talents | Treasures :: These are the resources God has entrusted each of us to steward well ::

Transparency :: Authenticity is required to build trust in Redemptive relationships, *which see* ::

Values; *also called* Six Values :: These values shape how our Church operates, living out our mission and vision; Worship | Learn | Connect | Serve | Give | Reach, *which see* ::

Vertical Relationship :: Our relationship with God; *see also* Horizontal ::

Victim :: Although we are victims of sin, we must understand that the primary issue is that we are also agents who have sinned against God and others; *see also* Agent ::

Vision :: Double Love Command, *which see* ::

Word of God :: Scripture, one of the primary ways God communicates with us; *see also* Spirit of God *and* People of God ::

Worship :: Our response of gratitude for who God is and what He does; one of the six Values, *which see* ::

NOTES

NOTES

www.ingramcontent.com/pod-product-compliance
Lightning Source LLC
Chambersburg PA
CBHW060622030426
42337CB00018B/3146